THE STORY BEHIND

PAPER

Barbara A. Somervill

www.raintreepublishers.co.uk
Visit our website to find out more information about Raintree books.

To order:
☎ Phone 0845 6044371
🖹 Fax +44 (0) 1865 312263
🖳 Email myorders@raintreepublishers.co.uk

Customers from outside the UK please telephone +44 1865 312262

Raintree is an imprint of Capstone Global Library Limited, a company incorporated in England and Wales having its registered office at 7 Pilgrim Street, London, EC4V 6LB – Registered company number: 6695582

Edited by Megan Cotugno and Diyan Leake
Designed by Philippa Jenkins
Original illustrations © Capstone Global Library Ltd 2011
Illustrated by Oxford Designers and Illustrators
Picture research by Hannah Taylor and Mica Brancic
Production by Eirian Griffiths
Originated by Capstone Global Library
Printed in China by CTPS

ISBN 978 1 406 22921 9 (hardback)
15 14 13 12 11
10 9 8 7 6 5 4 3 2 1

ISBN 978 1 406 22935 6 (paperback)
16 15 14 13 12
10 9 8 7 6 5 4 3 2 1

British Library Cataloguing in Publication Data
Somervill, Barbara A.
  The story behind paper. -- (True stories)
  676-dc22
A full catalogue record for this book is available from the British Library.

Acknowledgements
The author and publishers are grateful to the following for permission to reproduce copyright material: akg-images p. **6**; Alamy pp. **10** (© Interfoto), **16** (© Photobywayne), **19** (© Danita Delimont), **22** (© brt COMM); Alamy Image p. **21 bottom** (© The Art Gallery Collection); Corbis p. **9** (© Bettmann); Getty Images p. **8** (Hulton Archive); istockphoto p. **15** (© Paul Rodriguez); Photolibrary p. **23** (White/Harnett/Hanzon Harnett/Hanzon); Science Photo Library p. **13** (Power and Syred); Shutterstock pp. **4** (© Yildirim), **18** (© Dmitry Kalinovsky), **20** (© fotohunter), **24** (© Huguette Roe), **27** (© Anthony Hall), **21 top** (© Andrew Olscher), **iii** (© Discpicture), **11** (© Moreno Soppelsa), **26** (© design56); The Art Archive p. **7**.

Cover photograph of stack of crumpled papers reproduced with permission of Getty Images (Stone+/Paul Taylor).

We would like to thank Ann Fullick for her invaluable help in the preparation of this book.

Every effort has been made to contact copyright holders of material reproduced in this book. Any omissions will be rectified in subsequent printings if notice is given to the publisher.

Disclaimer
All the internet addresses (URLs) given in this book were valid at the time of going to press. However, due to the dynamic nature of the internet, some addresses may have changed, or sites may have changed or ceased to exist since publication. While the author and publisher regret any inconvenience this may cause readers, no responsibility for any such changes can be accepted by either the author or the publisher.

Contents

■ Paper all around us 4

■ The history of paper 6

■ How paper is made 12

■ Features of paper 16

■ Paper arts 19

■ Recycling paper 24

■ The future of paper 26

■ Timeline 28

■ Glossary 30

■ Find out more 31

■ Index 32

Some words are shown in bold, **like this**.
You can find out what they mean by
looking in the glossary.

Paper all around us

▲ **The day's news is printed on a type of paper called newsprint.**

We have paper all around us. Much of the food we eat is packaged in paper. We use wallpaper to cover our walls. We read newspapers, books, and magazines printed on paper, and we wipe up messes with paper towels. Students do homework in paper notebooks.

For fun, we read graphic novels, fly paper kites, and do arts and crafts projects with coloured card. We decorate bedroom walls with posters, and we record memories in scrapbooks. When the post comes, paper arrives in the form of bills, letters, advertisements, and birthday cards.

Most of this paper is made from wood **pulp**, which is produced by grinding up trees. Paper can also be made from cotton, linen, silk, or even rice and bamboo. Some paper is made from synthetic (human-made) materials, such as latex or plastic.

Uses for paper

Throughout the world, paper is used in hundreds of different ways. Canadian builders lay waterproof paper under roof shingles. Germans sell juice in waxed paper containers. The Chinese use rice paper for the beautiful art of writing called calligraphy – and for spring rolls, which are vegetables and pork or shrimp wrapped in rice paper and deep-fried. (Yes, people eat the paper!) The Japanese use a special paper, called *shoji gami*, to make sliding doors that separate rooms.

Paper money

Throughout the world, paper money is made with cloth **fibres** (pieces), which are strong and can take a lot of use. A British £5 note and a US$10 bill each last about three years before wearing out.

▼ **Brilliant red Chinese paper lanterns light up the night.**

The history of paper

▲ Ancient papers were mostly made with rags.

The word *paper* comes from *papyrus*, a kind of plant. The ancient Egyptians pounded papyrus into sheets and used it as a writing surface about 5,000 years ago. Papyrus was more like thin sheets of wood than paper, however.

Ancient China

The first people to make paper similar to the paper we use today were the Chinese. Evidence shows that the Chinese wrote on paper made from the fabric linen as early as 8 BC.

During the Han dynasty (202 BC–AD 220), Chinese paper was made from a mix of materials, including rags. In AD 105, a Chinese clerk named Ts'ai Lun pounded rags, fishnets, and the bark of a mulberry tree into pulp and pressed the pulp flat. When it dried, Ts'ai had writing paper.

Early Chinese paper was thicker and tougher than paper today. The heavy fibres made excellent clothing and, when several sheets were used together, it could even be used as armour in battle. The Chinese did not use paper as their main material for writing until about AD 200.

Trading paper

Paper, like silk and spices, was soon traded to other parts of the world. By 610 papermaking had spread north to Korea and Japan, and westward to India and Arab cultures. By the 700s, people in Baghdad, which is in present-day Iraq, had learned how to make paper. From Baghdad, papermaking reached Morocco, in North Africa, about 200 years later. Moroccan papermakers used **flax** and other plant fibres for pulp.

The first paper money

The Chinese began using paper money about 960 BC. Paper money replaced the need to carry heavy purses filled with coins.

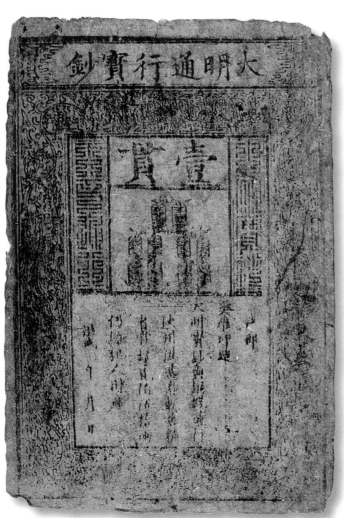

◀ Chinese people during the Sung dynasty (960 BC–AD 279) used paper money like this.

▲ **Early papermaking was done by hand.**

Paper in Europe

When paper finally reached Europe, around the 1000s, few people were interested in it. At that time, the Roman Catholic Church was very powerful. The Church thought paper was an Arab invention and did not want Catholics to use paper. Instead, the Church insisted on using **parchment** and **vellum**, which were both made from animal skins. In 1221 Holy Roman Emperor Frederick II said official documents written on paper were illegal. But paper was cheaper than parchment, and slowly people became interested in cheaper writing materials.

Italy

By 1100 Italy had become the papermaking centre of Europe. Italian papermakers developed pulp **mills**, which were large buildings dedicated to papermaking. Machines called **presses** helped to dry paper into flat sheets. The Italians also introduced wire screen **moulds** and presses. Finished paper was dried on ropes, like sheets on a clothes line.

Increased demand

In the 1200s and 1300s, books were very expensive. Each book had to be copied by hand, and Catholic religious men called monks handwrote most books over many months. In 1439 German inventor Johannes Gutenberg developed a **movable-type printing press**. Gutenberg's press made printing books faster. As the number of books printed increased, the demand for paper increased.

Papermakers continued to develop new, better, more efficient mill machinery. Europeans made beaters (much like today's food processors) to turn rags into pulp faster. They made finer moulds and better presses that used new kinds of machinery. Writing paper, newspapers, books, and magazines became part of the ever-growing demand for paper.

▼ Printing books increased the demand for paper.

9

▲ Papermaking was hard work in the 19th century.

Papermaking by machines

Beginning in the 1700s, the Industrial Revolution began. This was a time when power-driven machines replaced making products by hand. This brought many more changes to the paper **industry**. In 1798 British papermaker J. N. L. Robert developed the first flat-screen papermaking machine, which was a device that spread pulp smoothly on to a flat screen.

A few years later, French chemist Claude-Louis Berthollet discovered a way to bleach pulp and produce very white paper. Before Bertholett, paper was a pale brownish color, which made it more difficult to read the print.

At this time, rags were still often used to make paper. But in 1843 German inventor Friedrich Keller developed a machine that ground wood into pulp. From then on, wood-pulp paper replaced rag-made paper. Paper, once produced sheet by sheet, became larger, stronger, softer, and thinner. Papermaking changed from a skilled craft to an industry with factories.

Making paper in modern times

As mills expanded, paper companies bought forest land and began logging and **processing** their own wood. New machines were developed to make specific types of paper or cardboard. Photo paper (used for photographs) and waxed paper (used for food) were just two of the many new types of paper being produced.

In the 1900s, people became worried about how mills affected the **environment**. Water squeezed from the pulp and papermaking chemicals **polluted** rivers and soil. Smoke poured out of chimneys, polluting the air. Cutting down trees destroyed forests.

As a result, laws were passed to reduce pollution. Mills installed filters to reduce air and water pollution. Paper companies replanted forests, and people started **recycling**. Papermaking became more environmentally friendly.

▼ Today's paper mills produce paper by the ton.

How paper is made

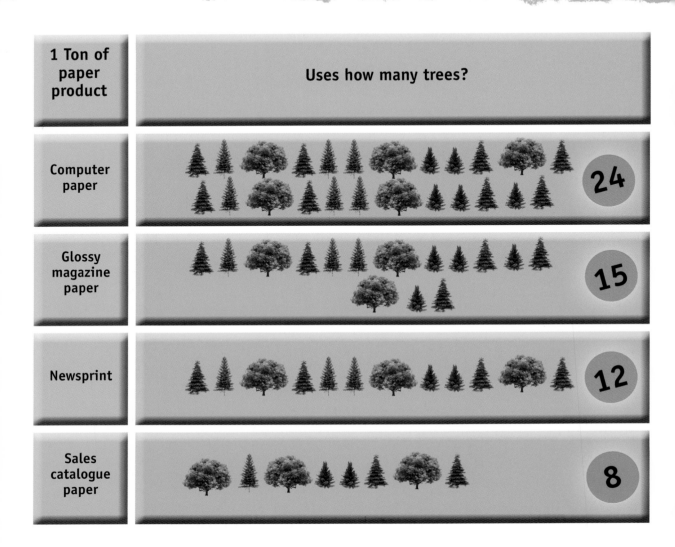

1 Ton of paper product	Uses how many trees?
Computer paper	24
Glossy magazine paper	15
Newsprint	12
Sales catalogue paper	8

▲ The type of paper determines the number of trees used to make that paper.

As we have seen, paper can be made from wood pulp. Wood is made of **cellulose**, the fibre that supports the internal structure of plants. **Hardwood** (maple and oak) pulp has short fibres and makes good writing paper. **Softwood** (pine and spruce) pulp has long fibres and makes stronger, rougher paper. Paper can also be made from cotton, linen, flax, silk, and different plant materials. Even grain stalks, such as wheat, make excellent paper pulp.

Harvesting wood

Today, most papermaking trees are farmed. When trees are harvested, new trees are planted in their place. Softwood trees grow relatively quickly. It takes about 15 years to grow a pine tree big enough to use for papermaking.

The basic recipe for paper is wood, water, and energy. The same ingredients make paper bags, soft facial tissues, children's colouring books, or glossy sports magazines.

Most countries have their own paper mills, but the United States is the world's largest paper producer. Japan, China, and Canada are also major paper producers. These countries all have vast forests for raw materials. Most paper mills use between 20 per cent and 100 per cent recycled paper to make pulp.

▼ Through a microscope you can see wood and other plant fibres in paper.

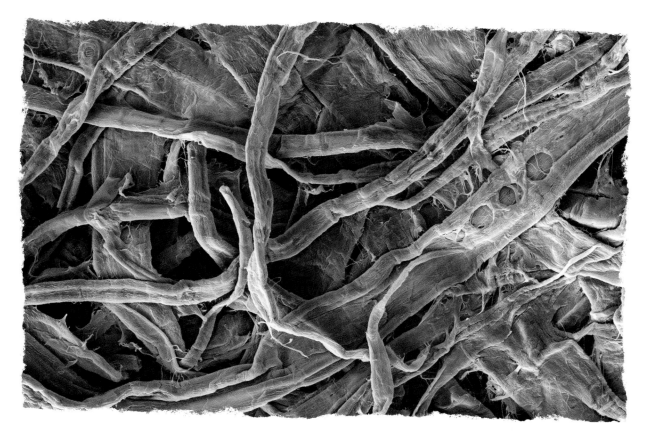

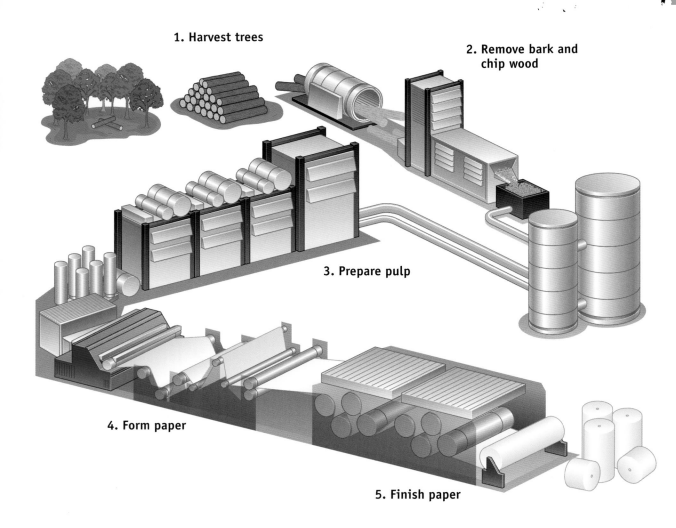

1. Harvest trees

2. Remove bark and chip wood

3. Prepare pulp

4. Form paper

5. Finish paper

▲ Papermaking machines turn timber to pulp to paper.

The paper process

Mills process logs by removing their bark. The wood is cleaned and run through a machine called a chipper. The chips are then ground down into wood pulp. Grinding separates the wood fibres. Water, other fibres, dyes for colour, and other chemicals are added and mixed into a mush.

Pulp made completely from trees is called **virgin wood pulp**. Pulp can also be made using part-virgin wood pulp and part-recycled paper. When the pulp mush is ready to be turned into paper, it contains about 99 per cent water.

From pulp to paper

To turn watery pulp into paper requires getting rid of the water. The wet mush is sprayed over fine screens, called wires. Rollers press the liquid mush flat, squeezing out the water. The rollers make sure the paper is smooth and of an even thickness. Then, the paper runs through a series of heated screens to dry it completely.

Wastewater is drained and recycled. Bits of fibre and chemicals are removed from the water. They are later burned to help power the paper mill. Cleaned water is used to make new pulp.

Finished paper

Finished paper is wound into large rolls that usually measure 9 metres (30 feet) long. A sharp cutter, called a slitter, cuts the rolls into shorter rolls. The rolls weigh more than 1.1 tons and are moved with a forklift.

▼ Dyes to make coloured paper are added to the pulp.

► Cardboard boxes are strong, to protect the materials inside.

Strength

For wrapping packages, paper needs to be strong. **Kraft paper** gets its name from the German word *Kraft*, meaning "strength". Kraft paper can be brown or bleached white, plain or waxed, or coated with plastic. Butchers use kraft paper for wrapping meat, and kraft paper is often used to make shopping bags. Plastic-coated kraft paper protects goods in storage and is used in construction and painting.

Cardboard can be thick sheets of paper, or it can be **corrugated**, meaning it has grooves. Regular cardboard is used to make boxes for packaging and book covers. Corrugated cardboard is made from two sheets of card, with a layer of grooved card in between. The grooves, called flutes, add strength. Corrugated cardboard makes strong boxes, ranging in size from folding parcel boxes to refrigerator cases.

Paper arts

Paper has many practical uses, but it can also be art. An artist adds flower petals and tiny leaves to pulp to make a unique sheet of paper. Nimble fingers fold a single sheet of green paper into a frog. An actor wears a **papier mâché** mask in a Greek play.

Papermaking is easy. When making handmade paper, artists recycle waste paper and fabrics to make pulp. Any material can be used – from jeans to old towels. Artists add dyes, flowers, leaves, and other fibres to add interest to their paper. If you want to try making paper, most craft stores sell papermaking kits.

▲ An artist collects just enough pulp in the frame to make a sheet of paper.

▲ Animals are a favourite subject for origami artists.

Origami

The key to **origami**, the Japanese art of folding paper, is making a figure using one piece of uncut paper. When paper first arrived in Japan, it was too expensive for everyday use. The Japanese originally made origami figures only for religious events. But from the 1600s to the 1800s, paper became common, and origami grew into a popular hobby. Today, origami pattern books offer instructions so that anyone can fold a crane, swan, or flower. Skilled origami artists create remarkably complex figures based on maths puzzles.

Papier mâché

Papier mâché is French for "chewed paper". But the art began in China as early as the Han dynasty (202 BC–AD 220). It involves making items using bits of paper and glue. Once dried and covered in a clear coating called lacquer, papier mâché is hard and hard-wearing. Typical papier mâché pieces include puppets, masks, fancy boxes, vases, and furniture.

Paper sculpture

Sculpting paper is not like carving wood or stone. In those arts, material is chipped away. With paper sculpting, paper is added to a base and shaped on a wire frame. The basic tools of paper sculpture are paper, scissors, and glue. One popular use for paper sculpture is making mobiles.

▲ These fruits and vegetables are papier mâché.

 Greetings cards

In the 1400s, Germans gave greeting cards to offer New Year's greetings. From then on, people began giving cards for Valentine's Day, Easter, Christmas, and birthdays. Victorian-era (1837–1901) greeting cards were very fancy, often with several layers of illustrated paper or moving paper parts.

▶ **Victorians gave their sweethearts very fancy Valentine's cards.**

21

A piece of *scherenschnitte* art has thousands of tiny scissor cuts.

Cut-paper art

Several cultures have turned cutting paper into art. The simplest cut-paper art is making snowflakes, which many children do. Slightly more difficult is making **silhouettes**, which were popular in Victorian times. A model sits between a light and a piece of paper. An artist traces the model's shadow and copies it onto black paper. The cut black paper forms a silhouette.

Only a skilled artist can create Japanese *kirie* or German *scherenschnitte*. The basic tools are paper, a design, and a sharp pair of scissors or art knife. The result of this artistry is like finely made lace.

Collage

Collage is the art of gluing paper and other materials against a background to produce a design or picture. The art of collage began in Japan in the 900s, when Japanese **calligraphers** began gluing bits of paper to their written documents. By the 1200s, monks in Europe added gold leaf, gems, and other items to their handwritten work. Coloured tissue paper is an ideal material for collage. Artists also use heavier, textured papers, photos, or magazine pictures.

 Soft, coloured tissue paper can be used to make a beautiful collage.

Marbleized paper

Marbleized paper has beautiful coloured patterns. Make some yourself! Put a thin layer of shaving cream on a baking tray. Add thin lines of food colouring across the shaving cream and swirl a fork through the colour. Lay a sheet of white paper on the shaving cream and press gently. Remove the sheet, scrape off the shaving cream, and lay the paper flat to dry.

The future of paper

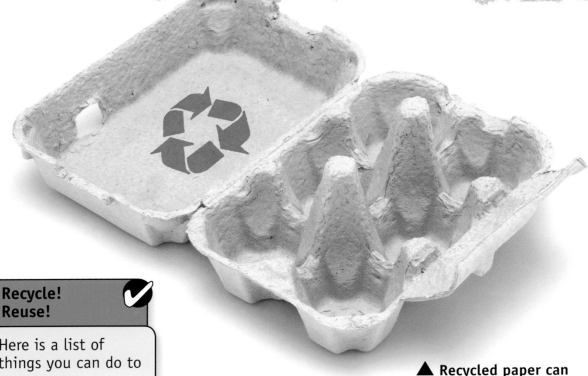

▲ Recycled paper can be used to make egg cartons.

Recycle! Reuse! ✔

Here is a list of things you can do to save paper:

- Use regular plates and glasses instead of paper plates.
- Recycle newspapers, magazines, phone directories, and junk mail.
- Use up the rest of half-used notebooks before buying new ones.
- Print on both sides of computer paper.
- Borrow books from the library instead of buying them.

Nearly one-third of all rubbish is paper or cardboard. Every 1.1 tons of paper recycled saves 30,000 litres (7,925 gallons) of water and 3,000 to 4,000 **kilowatt** hours of electricity. Using recycled paper to make new paper decreases air pollution by 95 per cent. Recycling also creates thousands of jobs – and saves thousands of trees.

The growth of recycling

Using recycled paper in papermaking is growing twice as fast as the use of virgin wood pulp. Paper is recycled more often than glass, aluminum, or plastic. In many countries, recycled paper is the only material used to make new paper.

Tomorrow's paper

Paper mills constantly develop new uses for paper. Scientists have created paper for packaging, paper plates, and paper cups that will rot away quickly in landfills. Intelligent paper packaging lets us see if products are past their sell-by dates by changing colour. Waterproof papers make excellent envelopes and also protect buildings from rain. Paper insulation is gaining popularity. And even batteries are being made from paper. The only limit to how we use paper in the future is our own imaginations.

▼ **Biodegradable cups break down in just 45 days.**

100% Biodegradable

Timeline

(These dates are often approximations.)

c. 3000 BC
Ancient Egyptians, Romans, and Greeks use papyrus as a writing surface.

3000 BC

AD 105
Chinese court official Ts'ai Lun makes writing paper from rags and other materials pressed together.

200   100

300   400

1100s
Moors introduce papermaking to Spain and Italy.

960
The Chinese begin using paper money.

1100   1000

1221
Holy Roman Emperor Frederick II declares that all official documents written on paper are illegal.

1282
The first watermarks – crosses and circles– are used in Italy to ensure documents are legal.

1390
Ulmann Stomer opens the first paper mill in Germany.

1200   1300

1804
The first book is printed on machine-made paper.

1798
British papermaker J. N. L. Robert develops the first flat-screen papermaking machine

1785
Claude-Louis Berthollet discovers a way to bleach pulp and produce very white paper.

1800 〰〰〰

1843
Friedrich Keller develops a machine that grinds wood into pulp.

1870
Robert Gair invents corrugated cardboard for boxes.

1904
The first paper plate is made.

1900

28   〰〰〰 This symbol shows where there is a change of scale in the timeline or where a long period of time with no noted events has been left out.

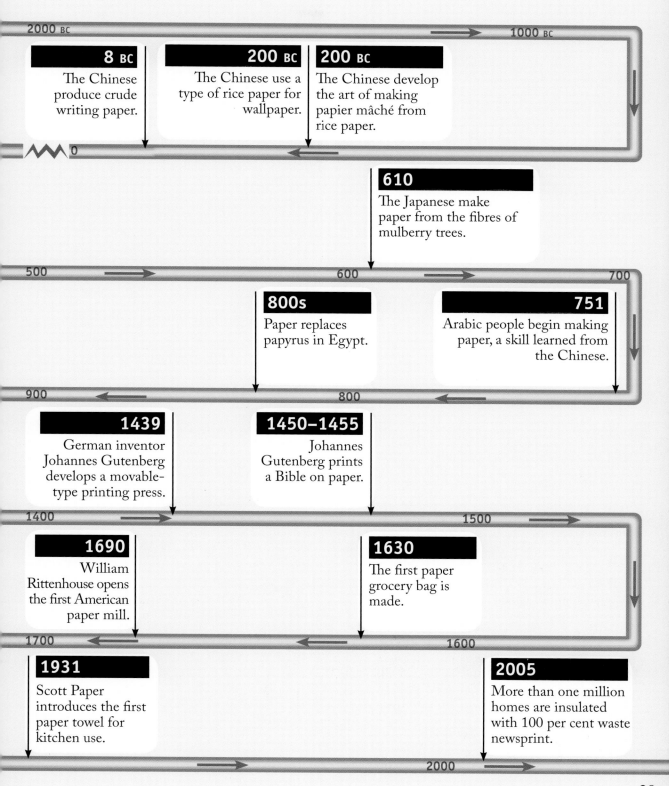

2000 BC ··· **1000 BC**

8 BC
The Chinese produce crude writing paper.

200 BC
The Chinese use a type of rice paper for wallpaper.

200 BC
The Chinese develop the art of making papier mâché from rice paper.

0

610
The Japanese make paper from the fibres of mulberry trees.

500 ··· **600** ··· **700**

800s
Paper replaces papyrus in Egypt.

751
Arabic people begin making paper, a skill learned from the Chinese.

900 ··· **800**

1439
German inventor Johannes Gutenberg develops a movable-type printing press.

1450–1455
Johannes Gutenberg prints a Bible on paper.

1400 ··· **1500**

1690
William Rittenhouse opens the first American paper mill.

1630
The first paper grocery bag is made.

1700 ··· **1600**

1931
Scott Paper introduces the first paper towel for kitchen use.

2005
More than one million homes are insulated with 100 per cent waste newsprint.

··· **2000** ···

Glossary

bale large bundle or package

calligrapher person who creates artistic handwritten texts

calligraphy fancy handwriting

cellulose material that makes up wood and the internal structure of plants

collage art made by gluing items to a background

corrugated made with ridges or grooves

environment air, water, minerals, and living things in an area

fibre piece of cloth or other material used in making paper

flax plant that produces fibres

gsm grams per square metre, or the weight of one sheet of paper that measures one metre by one metre

hardwood type of broad-leaved tree that grows dense wood, such as oak or cherry

industry large-scale production

insulation barrier to contain heat or cold

kilowatt measure of electricity use

kirie Japanese cut-paper art form

kraft paper heavy brown paper

mill factory for processing raw material

mill broke paper mill waste that has never been printed on

mould rigid frame covered with a screen on which pulp is pulled from the vat

movable type individual letters or characters that can be placed together to print a word or symbol

newsprint thin paper used for newspapers

origami Japanese art of folding paper

papier mâché craft material made from pulped paper and glue

papyrus reed used to make paper-like sheets

parchment writing material made from the skin of lambs or goats

pollute make the air, water, or soil unclean, usually with waste materials

post-consumer after having been used

press machine used to dry wet paper sheets so they dry flat

printing press machine used to place ink on paper or cloth

process actions for doing something

pulp cooked and beaten plant fibres, ready to be formed into sheets of paper

recycle renew, reuse, or process for another use

scherenschnitte cut-paper art form

shoji gami strong Japanese paper used for doors

silhouette outline of a shape

softwood type of coniferous tree that grows softer, pulpy wood, such as pine or cedar

synthetic made by humans, not nature

vellum writing material made from calfskin

virgin wood pulp pulp made from wood and without any recycled materials

watermark mark, such as a logo, hidden in paper

Find out more

Books

Paper (Re-using and Recycling), Ruth Thomson (Franklin Watts, 2006)

Papermaking (Step by Step), David Watson (Heinemann Library, 2000)

Paper Trail: History of an everyday material (Shockwave: Technology and Manufacturing), Susan Brocker (Children's Press, 2007)

A Piece of Paper: The science of materials and more (The Science In), Camilla de la Bédoyère (Franklin Watts, 2008)

Websites

Eco-friendly Kids
www.ecofriendlykids.co.uk/PaperMaking.html
Learn how to make paper the eco-friendly way – from recycled paper.

Origami That's Fun and Easy
www.origami-fun.com
Origami is an art everyone can enjoy. Learn how to do it at this website.

Pioneer Thinking: How to make paper
www.pioneerthinking.com/makingpaper.html
Visit this website to learn how to make paper.

Place to visit

The Paper Trail
Frogmore Mill
Fourdrinier Way
Apsley
Hemel Hempstead
Hertfordshire HP3 9RY
Tel: 01442 234600
www.thepapertrail.org.uk

Index

acid-free paper 16
art 5, 16, 19, 20, 21,
    22, 23

bales 24
beaters 9
Berthollet, Claude-
    Louis 10
bleaching 10, 18
bond grades 17
books 4, 9, 16, 20, 26

calligraphy 5, 23
Canada 5, 13
cardboard 11, 18, 26
cellulose 12
China 5, 6–7, 13, 20
chippers 14
coated paper 16, 18
collages 23
colours 10, 14, 23, 27
corrugated cardboard
    18
counterfeiting 17

demand 9

Egypt 6

fibres 5, 7, 12, 14, 15,
    19, 25
flat-screen
    papermaking 10
flutes 18
forests 11, 13
Frederick II (emperor)
    8

Germany 5, 9, 10, 21,
    22
Great Britain 5, 10
greeting cards 21
Gutenberg, Johannes 9

handmade paper 19
Han dynasty 6, 20
hardwood pulp 12

India 7
Industrial Revolution
    10
ingredients. See pulp.
insulation 25, 27
Italy 8, 17

Japan 5, 7, 13, 20, 22,
    23

Keller, Friedrich 10
kirie art 22
Korea 7
kraft paper 18

magazines 9, 12, 16, 23,
    25, 26
marbleized paper 23
materials. See pulp.
Middle East 7
mill broke 24
mills 8, 9, 10, 11, 13,
    14, 15, 24, 27
moulds 8, 9
money 5, 7
Morocco 7
movable-type printing
    press 9

newsprint 4, 9, 12, 17,
    26

official documents 8, 17
origami 20

packaging 4, 18, 27
papermaking 6, 7, 8, 9,
    10, 11, 12, 13, 14, 15,
    19, 24, 26
papier mâché 19, 20
papyrus 6
parchment 8
photo paper 11, 16
pollution 11, 26
post-consumer waste
    24
presses 8, 9
pulp 5, 6, 7, 8, 9, 10, 11,
    12, 13, 14, 15, 17, 19,
    24, 26

recycling 11, 13, 14, 15,
    19, 24, 25, 26
rice paper 5
Robert, J. N. L. 10
rollers 15
Roman Catholic
    Church 8, 9

scherenschnitte art 22
sculptures 21
silhouettes 22
slitters 15
snowflakes 22
softwood pulp 12, 13
strength 5, 10, 12, 18
synthetic materials 5

tissue paper 16, 23
trade 7
trash 26, 27
trees 5, 6, 11, 10, 11, 12,
    13, 14, 26
Ts'ai Lun 6

uncoated paper 17
United States 13, 17
uses 4, 5, 6, 7, 8, 9, 10,
    11, 12, 16–17, 18, 20,
    21, 23, 25, 27

vellum 8
virgin wood pulp 14, 26

water 11, 13, 14, 15,
    17, 26
watermarks 17
waterproof paper 5, 27
waxed paper 5, 11, 18
weight 17
wires 15
wood pulp. See trees;
    pulp.
writing paper 5, 6, 7, 8,
    9, 10, 12, 17, 23